SCARY SCOTTISH 'S

NASTY DEEDS AND SKULDUGGERY

DEBBIE JACKSON & MANDY SINCLAIR

For Gavin, with love
Debbie

To Scott, with love
Mandy

Designed by Melvin Creative

Printed in China

Published by

GW Publishing
PO Box 15070,
Dunblane,
FK15 5AN

www.gwpublishing.com

ISBN 978-0-9570844-3-8

CONTENTS

The castles in this book appear in order of a key event that took place there

CASTLE MACABRE

BATTLEMENTS
(AND WALL
WALK)

GUN HOLE

We're all bats round here

LAIRD'S
BEDCHAMBER

LADY'S
CHAMBER

GREAT HALL

A SCOTTISH
TOWER HOUSE

PRIVY

KITCHEN

DRAWBRIDGE

LAIRD'S PRIVATE
CHAMBER

STORES (CELLARS)

CHAPEL

POO

WELL

DUNGEON

BOTTLE
DUNGEON

POSTERN
(BACK DOOR
WITH IRON
YETT)

SMELLY MOAT

MOST BIG SCOTTISH CASTLES BEGAN WITH A TOWER HOUSE BUILT ON A HILL, A CLIFF, AN ISLAND
OR IN THE BEND OF A RIVER (MAKING IT HARDER FOR ENEMIES TO ATTACK). SOME HAD DRY MOATS
AND A FEW HAD MOATS FILLED WITH WATER.

INTRODUCTION

This book is about some of the great castles in Scotland. Each one has a unique story which is amazing, funny, terrible or sad. There are battles and sieges, dungeons and ghosts.

Travel back in time and discover the stories for yourself.

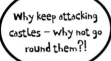

Why keep attacking castles – why not go round them?!

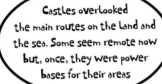

Castles overlooked the main routes on the land and the sea. Some seem remote now but, once, they were power bases for their areas

Robert the Moose answers your questions:

Who lived in all the castles?

This is how it worked:
Let's take King James IV. He had a small army. He was also in charge of all the land. He gave land and houses to nobles who supported him. The nobles gave smaller bits of land to their supporters who agreed, in return, to fight for (1) the king and (2) the noble
This was called man rent.

Did this work okay?

Sometimes. When the king needed a big army, the nobles brought their men to fight for him. But, if the nobles fell out with the king, they used their troops against him. If the nobles lost, though, they had their land taken away (and were probably killed)

Why did kings and queens keep travelling about?

They needed to be seen. To do this, they had to travel. They always took their household of nobles and servants with them – which could be hundreds of people. The roads were terrible so they went on horseback or by boat. Their possessions went by wagon. They moved between palaces – or might stay with a friendly noble

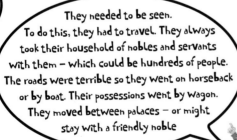

How did the friendly noble feel about that?

Terrible. He had to feed everyone

Good reasons for moving between houses a lot:

1. Be seen (avoiding 'out of sight, out of mind')
2. Keep an eye on the nobles
3. A chance for the last place to be cleaned
4. Cut down on disease (move on before the germs get you)
5. Save money (by staying with a noble)
6. Change of scenery
7. Something to do

ROTHESAY CASTLE 1230

Look out for Scottish places using Viking words!

Dal (dale) = valley, glen
Fjell (fell) = moorland or stony hill
Nes (ness) = headland
Vik (wick) = bay

ROTHESAY CASTLE, ON THE ISLE OF BUTE, WAS BUILT BY WALTER (STEWARD OF THE KING OF SCOTS) IN AROUND 1200.

IT WAS ON AN ISLAND, ON A HILL, WITH BIG THICK WALLS AND A MOAT AROUND IT – SO WALTER RECKONED HE WAS SAFE.

But, in 1230, Upsak the Viking besieged the castle for three days and then attacked it.

Upsak and his men won the battle and took the castle with all its treasure. (And there was lots of treasure!)

The Vikings had been on the Isle of Bute before.

Magnus III (King of Norway, Hebrides and Mann) built a wooden castle there.

I don't always have time to put my shoes on.

HE WAS ALSO CALLED MAGNUS BARELEGS →

Notice
Can you find Knut's sword? Over the years, it's found its way to 5 other castles...

How to pour hot oil onto your attackers:

1. Get lots of oil.

2. Heat it up (don't boil it or it might explode).

3. Carry the cauldron carefully.

4. Pour the oil down the walls.

AARGH! OUCH!

5. The oil will get under their armour.

7

What's a siege?

It's when an army surrounds a castle and won't let anyone in or out. When the people inside begin to starve, they have to surrender.

Sometimes the army gets fed up with waiting and storms the castle, using siege engines.

Clear orf

Shall we attack now?

VERY SMEL WATER

Hey, that's my lunch

Want to buy an apple?

CAERLAVEROCK MEANS: CASTLE OF THE SKYLARK.

STANDING CLOSE TO THE ENGLISH BORDER, CAERLAVEROCK WATCHED OVER TWO IMPORTANT WATERWAYS. THE CASTLE WAS SURROUNDED BY MARSHES WITH A TIDAL RIVER BESIDE IT. IT WAS IMPOSSIBLE TO TAKE THIS FORTRESS BY SURPRISE. INSTEAD, ARMIES BESIEGED IT.

In 1300, King Edward I of England laid siege to the castle with 3,000 men and 87 knights. He brought siege engines with him.

Aargh!

Warwolf was used to attack Caerlaverock Castle.

EDWARD'S MEN TOOK CONTROL OF THE CASTLE BUT THE SCOTS GOT IT BACK AGAIN 12 YEARS LATER.

WARWOLF

If you wanted to attack a castle - but could only buy one siege engine - which would you choose?

☑ Trebuchet
Good: you can hurl huge stones, dead animals, people's heads, things on fire, etc over castle walls
Bad: it can be scary

☐ Siege tower
Good: you can use it to climb over big walls
Bad: it's huge and heavy

☐ Battering ram
Good: you can knock down big wooden gates
Bad: it's rubbish for iron gates

☐ Petard
Good: you can blow up castles
Bad: you've got to tunnel under the walls first

is cave, at all. ←

A FEW MILES FROM BRODICK CASTLE, IS THE KING'S CAVE. IT'S SAID THAT ROBERT THE BRUCE HID THERE. HE WAS EXHAUSTED, AND NEAR TO GIVING UP, WHEN SOMETHING HAPPENED TO RESTORE HIS SPIRITS.

There are two stories:

1. He met a woman who could see into the future. She told him that he would free Scotland from the enemy. Her two sons joined him to fight.

2. He met a spider in the cave who was trying to weave a web. The web kept breaking but the spider kept on trying until, finally, it held. Bruce took this as a sign. He knew that he should keep on trying, too.

DO YOU THINK THESE STORIES ARE TRUE?

AT THAT TIME, KING EDWARD I OF ENGLAND HAD INVADED SCOTLAND. HIS ARMY HELD MANY SCOTTISH CASTLES, INCLUDING BRODICK.

In 1307, Bruce's band of men took back Brodick Castle

It was one of the first castles to be re-captured by the Scots

Seven years later, Bruce's troops beat Edward II's army of English, Welsh, Irish, French and Scotsmen at Bannockburn!

We could be descended from Bruce's famous spider!

Darling, you'll never guess what I can see

The white stag

The Hamilton family once owned Brodick Castle. Whenever a chief of the Hamilton clan was close to death, a white stag appeared.

I'd rather not know

11

DOUNE CASTLE 1400

DOUNE WAS ONCE AN INCREDIBLY STRONG CASTLE. IT WAS SET ON A HIGH RIDGE OF LAND, WITH **MASSIVE WALLS** AND A HUGE GATEHOUSE! FEW ATTACKERS EVER MANAGED TO GET INSIDE.

Did you know?
Mary Queen of Scots stayed here.
Bonnie Prince Charlie and his troops dropped by.
Monty Python and the Holy Grail was filmed here!

Shall we go home?

Attackers! Would you rather:

1. Race up this hill and climb our 10 metre walls while we pour boiling oil over you?

OR

2. Storm our gatehouse, fight your way through the big wooden gate, the portcullis, the iron yett, up the long steep tunnel and through another iron yett - while we shoot arrows and hit you with our swords?

Aye

ZZZZZZ

THE JACOBITES HELD JOHN WITHERSPOON PRISONER AT DOUNE IN 1746. JOHN WASN'T KEEN ON BONNIE PRINCE CHARLIE (OR ANY PRINCE OR KING, REALLY). LATER, JOHN WENT TO AMERICA. HE WAS ONE OF THE PEOPLE WHO SIGNED AMERICA'S DECLARATION OF INDEPENDENCE.

Which American actress is descended from John Witherspoon?

I say: Let everyone be equal.

Does that include rats?

Answer: Reese Witherspoon

13

ROBERT THE BRUCE (THE SIMPLE VERSION)

1. HE WAS BORN AT TURNBERRY CASTLE, AYRSHIRE IN 1274.
2. HE FOUGHT AGAINST KING EDWARD I OF ENGLAND.
3. HE KILLED HIS SCOTTISH RIVAL JOHN COMYN IN A CHURCH AT DUMFRIES.
4. HE WAS CROWNED KING OF SCOTLAND AT SCONE IN 1306.
5. HE FOUGHT AGAINST KING EDWARD II OF ENGLAND.
6. HE BEAT EDWARD II'S HUGE ARMY (ABOUT 18,000 MEN) AT THE BATTLE OF BANNOCKBURN IN 1314.
7. THIS LED TO SCOTLAND BECOMING A UNITED AND INDEPENDENT COUNTRY.
8. HE DIED IN 1329. HIS SON AND THEN HIS DAUGHTER'S SON RULED SCOTLAND.
9. IN 1603, HIS DESCENDANT KING JAMES VI ALSO BECAME JAMES I OF ENGLAND.
10. THE PRESENT MONARCH IS DESCENDED FROM ROBERT THE BRUCE, THROUGH KING JAMES VI.

BATTLE OF BANNOCKBURN. THE SCOTTISH SCHILTRONS STOPPED EDWARD'S WAR HORSES.

SCOTTISH HOUSE OF BRUCE & STEWART FAMILY TREE

Robert I the Bruce + Isobella of Mar
1274-1329 *(King from 1306)*

Marjorie Bruce + Walter Stewart
1296-1316

- (Robert II's uncle David II was king from 1329-1371)

Robert II + Elizabeth Mure
1316-1390 *(King from 1371)*

Robert III + Annabella Drummond
1340-1406 *(King from 1390)*

James I + Joan Beaufort
1394-1437 *(King from 1406)*

James II + Mary of Guelders
1430-1460 *(King from 1437)*

James III + Margaret of Denmark
1451-1488 *(King from 1460)*

James IV + Margaret Tudor (Daughter of Henry VII)
1473-1513 *(King from 1488)*

James V + Mary of Guise
1512-1542 *(King from 1513)*

Mary I Queen of Scots + Henry Lord Darnley
1542-1587 *(Queen from 1542 to 1567)*

James VI + Anne of Denmark
1566-1625 *(King from 1567)*
James VI also became James I of England in
1603 upon the death of Elizabeth I

Bannockburn was the bigger and best battle. We got back Stirling Castle and routed Edward's army. It wasn't the end of his threat but it was the beginning of the end

EDINBURGH CASTLE 1440

EDINBURGH CASTLE IS THE MOST FAMOUS OF ALL THE SCOTTISH CASTLES. IT BECAME THE KING'S OFFICIAL HOME IN THE 1400s, WHEN KING JAMES II MADE EDINBURGH THE CAPITAL OF SCOTLAND.

DUKE OF ALBANY

The castle is on a great mound, with cliffs on three sides. Everyone thought that the cliffs would stop people from breaking into (or out of) the castle. But they were wrong.

Going Up

- 30 soldiers climbed up to surprise 350 knights loyal to King Edward I of England.

Going Down

- 1 Duke who slid down a rope and climbed down the rock face.
- 4 men who used washing lines.
- 49 prisoners who cut a hole in a wall (one was re-captured).
- 1 man who hid in a dung barrow – but he got tipped over the cliff edge with the dung.

How many escaped?

> Quelle horreur! Il est terrible!

Mary Queen of Scots' mum is said to **haunt** the palace. She's a bit grumpy because, when she died, her body was left for **three months** before being sent to France for burial!

MARY OF GUISE

Edinburgh Castle has:

- A huge cannon called Mons Meg!
- The Coronation Stone!!
- The Crown Jewels!!!
- The Laird's Lug (what?)

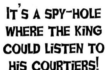

IT'S A SPY-HOLE WHERE THE KING COULD LISTEN TO HIS COURTIERS!

The Black Dinner

In the 1400s, the Douglas family were very powerful and the other nobles didn't like it. So they got 10-year-old King James II to invite the 6th Earl of Douglas and his brother to a very special dinner. There the Earl was served a dish containing the severed head of a black bull. This was a symbol of death. The Douglas brothers sprang up and tried to defend themselves but were quickly over-powered. James asked that the brothers be spared but to no avail. They were dragged away - to suffer the same fate as the bull.

GLAMIS CASTLE c.1486

GLAMIS HAS BEEN A FAMILY HOME SINCE 1372. IT'S BEEN CALLED THE **MOST HAUNTED HOUSE** IN BRITAIN! THE GHOSTS INCLUDE LORD GLAMIS AND THE GREY LADY.

Glamis = say 'Glams'

Their secret room is within the great walls of the crypt.

Tis the Devil himself!

Here's the story of Lord Glamis:

The laird of Glamis often played cards and gambled with his friends, including his great rival the Earl of Crawford. They never played on a Sunday though. Gambling on the Sabbath was considered a sin. However, one Saturday evening, Lord Glamis and the Earl were deep into a game as the clock struck midnight. Their friends begged them to stop but Lord Glamis cried out merrily, "Let's play until Doomsday!" He threw a card upon the table and, at that moment, the Devil appeared. "You have your wish!" he said, "You shall indeed play until Doomsday."

18

Lots of important people have visited Glamis.

No one can get into the room anymore - but you may hear them wailing and still playing cards!

Um — I didn't mean what I said earlier...

I'm out of here

MARY, QUEEN OF SCOTS

KING JAMES V

SHAKESPEARE

Who visits your home?

I like your dog

THE QUEEN MOTHER, ELIZABETH BOWES-LYON (IT WAS HER CHILDHOOD HOME)

Macbeth

William Shakespeare's play about Macbeth is set at Glamis: Macbeth, Thane of Glamis, kills King Duncan. (That wasn't really true — but a play needn't stick to facts!) There really was a Macbeth, and he would have known Glamis. The play is famous for its witches.

Macbeth

So foul and fair a day I have not seen

The Grey Lady

In the chapel at Glamis, one seat is always kept free for the Grey Lady. She is thought to be the ghost of Janet Douglas, widow of the 6th Lord Glamis. She was wrongly accused of witchcraft by King James V (who hated the Douglas family) and, in 1537, she was **burnt to death.**

19

EILEAN DONAN CASTLE 1488

EILEAN DONAN CASTLE STANDS ON A SMALL ISLAND IN LOCH DUICH. IT WAS ONCE OWNED BY THE MACKENZIES – BUT THE MACRAES LIVED THERE FOR MANY YEARS. THEY WERE **A WARRIOR CLAN** AND RECOGNISED MACKENZIE AS THEIR CHIEF.

The Big Fight:

The Mackenzies' main enemy was the Macdonald clan. In 1488, at a place called The Park, there was a great fight. Duncan Macrae (also called Big Duncan of **the Battleaxe**) fought the Macdonald's champion warrior, called MacLaine of Lochbuie.

Duncan won. But that didn't stop the feud. It went on for another 50 years!

Squelch!

Aargh!

BOOOM!

In 1719, when King George I was on the British throne, Spanish soldiers took over the castle in support of the Jacobites. But then three Government ships appeared in the loch and **blew the castle up.**

Castle as it is today

Eilean Donan was a ruin for about 200 years until John MacRae-Gilstrap restored it. It took him 20 years — but now everyone can visit. It has become the **most iconic castle** in Scotland.

Eilean Donan was built for left-handed warriors. Visit the castle and find out why!

THE CASTLE WITH THE FAIRY TOWER

How long have you lived in your home?

The clan chief had his own piper.

Marvellous

Yikes!

MR MacCRIMMON

The Potato Famine

In the 1800s, most poor people relied on potatoes for their main food but, in 1847, the potatoes became diseased and **rotten**. A great famine lasted for five years. Some clan chiefs ignored their people – or even cleared them from their land. But the 25th Chief Norman MacLeod offered his clan food and work. He fell into debt and **rented out the castle**, moving to London to work as a clerk. It wasn't until 1929 that the 27th Chief could return to Dunvegan Castle.

DUNVEGAN IS ON THE ISLE OF SKYE. IT'S BEEN THE HOME OF THE CLAN MACLEOD CHIEFS FOR NEARLY **800** YEARS.

It's famous for its Fairy Flag

I hate midges

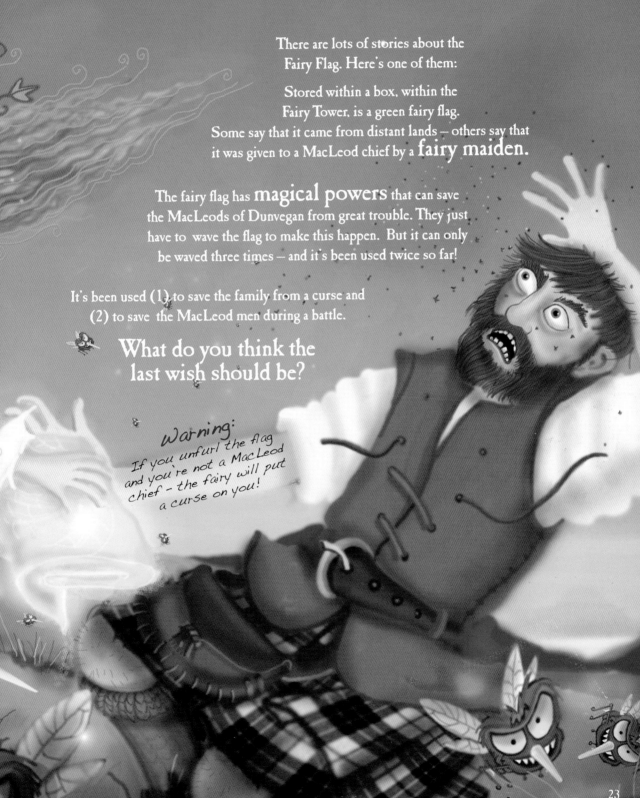

DUNVEGAN CASTLE c.1500

There are lots of stories about the
Fairy Flag. Here's one of them:

Stored within a box, within the
Fairy Tower, is a green fairy flag.
Some say that it came from distant lands — others say that
it was given to a MacLeod chief by a **fairy maiden.**

The fairy flag has **magical powers** that can save
the MacLeods of Dunvegan from great trouble. They just
have to wave the flag to make this happen. But it can only
be waved three times — and it's been used twice so far!

It's been used (1) to save the family from a curse and
(2) to save the MacLeod men during a battle.

What do you think the
last wish should be?

Warning:
If you unfurl the flag
and you're not a MacLeod
chief - the fairy will put
a curse on you!

BEST DRESSED KNIGHT

1 Helm
2 Chainmail
3 Spaulders
4 Gauntlet
5 Kneecup
6 Greave
7 Soloret

VIEW
THROUGH
A HELM

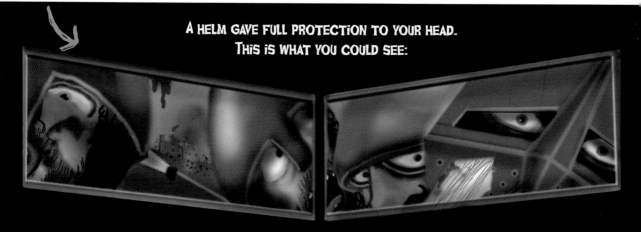

A HELM GAVE FULL PROTECTION TO YOUR HEAD.
THIS IS WHAT YOU COULD SEE:

COAT OF ARMS

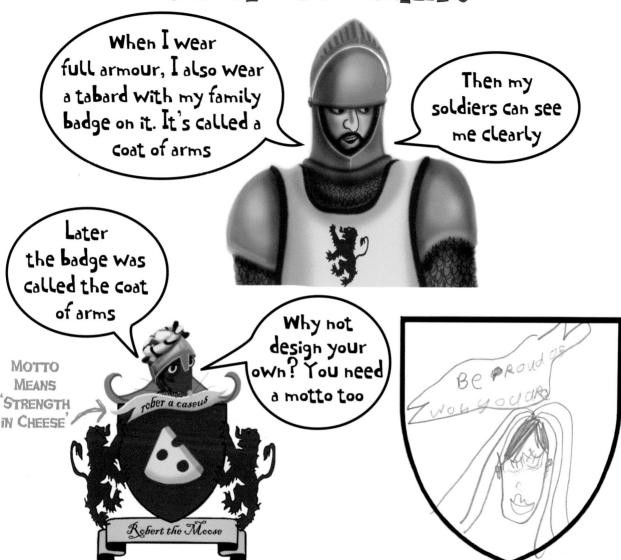

When I wear full armour, I also wear a tabard with my family badge on it. It's called a coat of arms

Then my soldiers can see me clearly

Later the badge was called the coat of arms

Why not design your own? You need a motto too

MOTTO MEANS 'STRENGTH IN CHEESE'

rober a caseus

Robert the Moose

Be proud os wob you are

JUMBLED WORDS

THESE ARE ALL THINGS BELONGING TO THE KNIGHT. CAN YOU UN-JUMBLE THE WORDS?

1. emhl   *nolm*
2. necpuke
3. dowrs

4. aveger
5. uttlegans
6. rootels

7. himlicaan
8. howserra
9. prassulde

Answers: 1.helm 2.kneecup 3.sword 4.greave 5.gauntlets 6.soleret 7.chainmail 8.warhorse 9.spaulders

25

LINLITHGOW PALACE 1510

Linlithgow was built by the Stewart kings, starting with King James I in 1424. It stood on the road between the huge (AND DRAUGHTY) royal castles of Edinburgh and Stirling. Although a grand palace, Linlithgow was also a comfortable home with lovely gardens and lots of FRESH COUNTRY AIR. It was much loved by the royal families.

Take that!

This is a daft sport

Lots of people spoke Gaelic in those days. James IV was the last Scottish monarch to speak it!

Several babies were born at the palace, including Mary Queen of Scots. Her son became King James VI of Scotland. In 1603, he also became James I of England and moved his court to London. Linlithgow Palace fell into disrepair and, in 1745, its lovely old rooms were destroyed in a big fire

CLUNK!

King James IV often stayed at Linlithgow. A favourite sport, in those days, was jousting. It could be very dangerous. They stopped jousting in France after their king got killed!

Watch out

Where can he be?

MARGARET TUDOR

James IV married Margaret Tudor. She was the daughter of King Henry VII of England. The two countries signed a peace treaty, but James later invaded England in support of the Auld Alliance with France.

James was killed, along with many Scottish nobles, at the Battle of Flodden in 1513. It's said that 10,000 men died there. An old Scottish folk song, Flowers of the Forest, became the lament for Flodden.

If you visit Linlithgow Palace, look out for this mason s mark in one of the rooms! (When stonemasons built fine buildings, they often left their own special mark somewhere.)

DUART CASTLE c.1520

Duart Castle is on the Isle of Mull. It's the home of Clan Maclean. It's one of a chain of castles along the coast that once guarded the Sound of Mull. The first stone keep was built in about 1370. The walls were over 3 metres thick.

Back in those days, there were no real roads, just tracks. This meant that travelling by boat was very important. The Sound of Mull was one of the busiest routes around Scotland.

Lachlan Cattanach (11th Chief of the Clan) married Catherine Campbell but they didn't have any children.

This made him SO cross that he put his wife on a rock in the sea and waited for the high tide to drown her. Luckily, a passing fisherman saved her and took her back to her family home.

Not realising this, Lachlan visited her brother, the Earl of Argyll, to tell him that she was dead – only to find her sitting beside the Earl!

Lachlan was stabbed to death in his bed about two years later, probably by one of his wife's brothers.

When soldiers watched for enemy ships, they sometimes lit beacons that sent signals along the coast.

How to use a beacon:

1. Climb a big hill and make a huge fire. This may take some time.

2. Take a rest and watch out for other beacons.

3. When you see one (fire on distant hill), light your fire.

Something fishy is going on...

4. Wait for next beacon to be lit. Then hide.

EACHUIN THE HEADLESS GHOST (SON OF IAIN "THE TOOTHLESS" MACLAINE OF LOCH BUIE).

THE CASTLE IS ON DUBH ARD (THE BLACK POINT).

A keep is a tower with very thick walls.

STIRLING CASTLE 1541

STIRLING CASTLE IS SET **HIGH ON A CRAGGY HILL** ABOVE THE TOWN OF STIRLING AND THE FORTH VALLEY. IT CAN BE SEEN FOR MILES AROUND. IN MEDIEVAL TIMES, ITS POSITION WAS IMPORTANT FOR ANY ARMY BECAUSE IT OVERLOOKED THE MAIN ROUTE BETWEEN THE LOWLANDS AND HIGHLANDS.

In 1538,

King James V built a palace within the castle walls, and turned the fortress into a modern royal home. The new building was beautiful. It had all the latest features and décor. The royal party enjoyed staying there - but it was **hard work** for the servants because they had to feed hundreds of people!

The Flying Alchemist

James IV had an alchemist called John Damien. His job was to turn metal into gold. He failed, so he **decided to fly** instead. Wearing a large pair of wings, he leapt from the castle walls – and fell into a midden. He lived but broke his leg.

A quick history on: The Jameses!

- These Stewart monarchs all stayed at Stirling Castle. They weren't always happy though.
- King James I beheaded some of his rivals on the beheading hill, nearby. He was **murdered**.
- King James II fell out with the Earl of Douglas and **stabbed** him to death in the castle.
- King James III fell out with his wife and son, and was **assassinated** nearby.
- King James IV was **liked** by most of his subjects (which was a surprise after the first three kings). He built the Great Hall and invited lots of poets and musicians to the castle.
- King James V had one living child, called **Mary**. She was later crowned Queen of Scots.
- Mary Queen of Scots **fell in love** with her cousin Henry Darnley at Stirling Castle. They married and had a son. There's more about Mary at Falkland Palace!

The locals called it 'the ship that never sailed'. Can you see why?

KEEPER'S HOUSE

PRISON TOWER

GUN HOLE

ANGLED WALLS

WALL 3M THICK

PIT DUNGEON

SEA

I canna feel ma toes!

Tis freezin!

CROAK

The pit dungeon flooded twice a day at high tide, which kept it nice and clean.

Get me out of here. I'm a celebrity!

PRISON TOWER RESERVED FOR RICH/IMPORTAN PRISONERS

CARDINAL BEATON

Um... interesting... stonework

Aye

Must be time for a wee snack soon

BLACKNESS CASTLE 1543

BLACKNESS CASTLE WAS BUILT IN THE 1440s BY SIR GEORGE CRICHTON. (HE WAS A VERY POWERFUL MAN AND SOME PEOPLE DIDN'T LIKE HIM). HE TOLD KING JAMES II THAT HIS NEW CASTLE WAS AN AMAZINGLY STRONG FORTRESS. THE KING AGREED AND ASKED TO HAVE IT. SO IT BECAME A ROYAL FORTRESS!

Blackness was the seaport for Linlithgow Palace. It was also just 14 miles down the coast from Edinburgh Castle. The King's men at Blackness Castle could keep an eye on all ships that sailed up the River Forth.

Sir James Hamilton of Finnart made the castle even stronger for King James V (who was his second cousin) but he fell out with the king and lost his head in 1540. The work at Blackness was completed in 1543.

This is the very latest sort of castle. It's the king's strongest one

Very nice

PIT DUNGEON, WITH WATER FEATURE. RESERVED FOR POOR PRISONERS

CASTLE KEEPER'S HOME KEPT READY IN CASE ROYAL FAMILY VISIT

HOW TO BE A WITCH (IN MEDIEVAL TIMES)

1. MOST WITCHES ARE WOMEN.

2. IT'S BETTER TO LOOK OLD.

3. YOU MIGHT WEAR SLIGHTLY ODD CLOTHES.

4. TRY LIVING ALONE – AND IN A WOOD.

5. OWN A BLACK OR BRINDLED CAT.

6. YOU NEED A DEVIL'S MARK – A PIMPLE WILL DO.

7. IF YOU'RE A MEDICINE WOMAN, THAT'S PERFECT.

If that doesn't work, try leaping out in front of someone and shrieking: I put a curse on you! All your piglets will have five legs

BRINDLED CAT

WITCHFINDERS' MANUAL

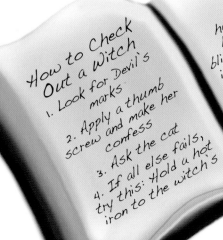

How to Check Out a Witch
1. Look for Devil's marks
2. Apply a thumb screw and make her confess
3. Ask the cat
4. If all else fails, try this: Hold a hot iron to the witch's hand. If her hand blisters, she's innocent. But if it heals quickly, or leaves no mark, then burn her on a big fire

Witch Required
Apply Within
Mainly night work.
Must be good at cooking, flying and chanting.
And not mind toads.

THE WITCHES' BREW WORDSEARCH

SHAKESPEARE'S PLAY MACBETH IS SET IN SCOTLAND.
MACBETH IS THE THANE OF GLAMIS AND CAWDOR.
THE 3 WITCHES IN THE PLAY MAKE A MAGIC BREW.

Hubble bubble toil and trouble...

Here's some of the ingredients

```
L D D E H W C A L Y V A Z V S
Z P R R B Q O G O A T B I L E
S Y A E W C F L O R H H I S D
E L G I P F N K F A Q A R F H
V I O B Y H W D M T R P N Y F
A Z N W A D D E R T O N G U E
E A S O W L W I N G E O O T U
L R C J E O G E V L F Z T N G
W D A T O O R K C O L M E H N
E L L B T E V M U O O Y Z K O
Y E E H G P I B S W E D R S T
M G O I O S D A O T D L O C G
A M T N R K A A W A I M R U O
D F U Z F L X E D B A N F D D
Y B A B O O N B L O O D G T L
```

Can you find them?

ADDER TONGUE	HEMLOCK ROOT
BABOON BLOOD	LIZARD LEG
BAT WOOL	NEWT EYE
COLD TOAD	OWL WING
DOG TONGUE	SLOWWORM STING
DRAGON SCALE	TIGER ENTRAILS
FROG TOE	WOLF TOOTH
GOAT BILE	YEW LEAVES

I wish they'd stick to chocolate brownies

ST. ANDREWS CASTLE 1547

ST. ANDREWS CASTLE IS A RUIN NOW BUT WAS ONCE THE HOME OF BISHOPS AND ARCHBISHOPS WHO WERE VERY POWERFUL PEOPLE.

In 1546, George Wishart was **burnt at the stake** at St Andrews. George was a Protestant leader. Being a Protestant was quite new in those days. Up until then people had always been Catholic but new ideas had recently arrived from Europe. The Protestants were really cross about George getting burnt so they took St Andrews Castle and refused to give it back. (They also stabbed the Archbishop to death).

This made the Catholics really cross so they besieged the castle. Next, a fleet of French ships arrived. The French supported the Catholics so they **bombarded the castle**. The Protestants had to give in and were sent to galleys in the French fleet.

Gotcha!

Aargh!

WANTED:
TUNNELERS
Need to be:
1. Very strong
2. Good at digging
3. Good at setting mines
4. Like dark underground places
5. Don't mind getting buried (maybe)

While the seige was on, Catholic miners tunnelled beneath the castle walls. They wanted to plant mines and **blow up the walls**. But counter-miners, from the Protestant side, tunnelled out and stopped them.

If you visit the castle, you can still see the mines and the bottle dungeon

Can I come out now?

Make it quick

GEORGE WISHART

What you're hoping for at this point:

1. They can't light the fire
2. They change their minds
3. Someone has a big bucket of water
4. Or the fire burns quickly

St Andrews has a **very deep** bottle dungeon. You definitely don't want to be stuck in a bottle dungeon.

Has anyone got a light?

A PROTESTANT (in 1546): A CHRISTIAN WHO NO LONGER BELIEVED IN THE ROMAN CATHOLIC CHURCH.

FALKLAND PALACE 1562

In Scotland, rich families could only hold land if the King or Queen said so. In 1525, the Earl of Fife upset King James II by (probably) MURDERING HIS BROTHER. As a punishment, the King took Falkland Castle off him.

The old castle was re-built by Kings James IV and James V. They made it into a very fashionable palace.

James V was Mary Queen of Scots' father, but he died at the palace just six days after she was born. Mary became Queen of Scotland.

Mary was sent to France when she was just five years old and married her childhood friend, Francis, at the age of 15. He became King of France but, sadly, he died a year later. In 1561, Mary returned to Scotland.

Mary Queen of Scots. The good, the b...

MARY WAS VERY CLEVER AND PRETTY, SPOKE SEVERAL LANGUAGES AND WAS GOOD AT SPORTS.

What would you like to do today, your Highness?

She would've made a great school captain!

d the dreadful

What are you good at?

The good...

Mary loved visiting Falkland Palace. It was somewhere she could **relax**.

I'm really good at:

1. ....
2. ....
3. ....

The bad...

Mary married twice more. Her second husband (Henry Darnley) was **murdered**. Her third husband (James Bothwell) was much **hated** and the people turned against her.

She fled to England and sought refuge with her cousin. But her cousin, Queen Elizabeth I, put her under house arrest.

The dreadful...

Mary wanted to return to Scotland but her infant son James had been made king. The men who were in charge of him didn't want her around. She **never saw her son again**. Mary stayed under house arrest for 18 years. In 1587, a plot against Queen Elizabeth was discovered and Mary was blamed. She was **beheaded** at Fotheringay Castle.

DIRLETON CASTLE 1585

DIRLETON CASTLE WAS KNOWN AS A COMFORTABLE CASTLE WITH FINE GARDENS. IT WAS ABOUT TWENTY MILES FROM EDINBURGH.

IN 1585, THE PLAGUE BROKE OUT IN EDINBURGH. THE PLAGUE WAS ALSO CALLED **THE BLACK DEATH** BECAUSE PEOPLE GOT HUGE BOILS AND LOTS OF BLACK SPOTS. AFTER THIS, THEY GOT VERY, VERY SICK – AND WERE OFTEN **DEAD BEFORE BED-TIME.**

King James VI and his courtiers fled from the city to find a safer place to stay. He decided to visit his friend the Earl of Arran, at Dirleton Castle.

In 1649, the Witchfinder John Kincaid visited some servants at Dirleton Castle. They'd been accused of **Devil worship.** Sure enough, Kincaid found Devil's marks upon them – so they were burnt at the stake, by order of the Parliament.

A FISHER WOMAN BROUGHT THE PLAGUE TO EDINBURGH

What?

Forsooth! It be a Devil's mark...

Tis a pimple!

40

Also in 1649, King Charles I was **beheaded** in London. The next year, Cromwell's troops under General Monck brought siege engines to Dirleton Castle and destroyed it.

CASTLE CAMPBELL 1644

CASTLE CAMPBELL WAS ONCE CALLED CASTLE GLOOM BUT, WHEN THE CAMPBELL FAMILY GOT IT, THEY DIDN'T LIKE ITS NAME. SO THEY CALLED IT AFTER THEMSELVES. THAT WAY EVERYONE KNEW WHO OWNED IT.

CASTLE CAMPBELL STANDS HIGH ABOVE A CHASM (A DEEP GAP IN THE HILLSIDE). IN THE GAELIC LANGUAGE, 'GLOM' MEANS CHASM. TWO RIVERS MEET BELOW THE CASTLE: THE BURN OF CARE AND THE BURN OF SORROW.

ARCHIBALD CAMPBELL, 1ST MARQUESS OF ARGYLL. HE WAS A STRICT COVENANTER.

In the 1640s, Archibald Campbell lived at the castle. He was a man who **couldn't make up his mind.** At first he supported King Charles I – but then decided he didn't like him anymore. So then he supported King Charles II – until he fell out with him. In the end, he supported Oliver Cromwell who didn't like any kings at all.

Cheerful round here, isn't it?

WHY I KEEP CHANGING MY MIND, BY ARCHIBALD CAMPBELL

I DON'T APPROVE OF THE STUART KINGS' LIFESTYLE.

I RATHER FANCY RULING SCOTLAND MYSELF.

FIND OUT MORE ABOUT ARCHIBALD AND CHARLES AT SCONE PALACE

Would you rather be a Covenanter or a Royalist?

Here's the top 5 musts:

Covenanters:

1. Support more equality
2. Have a nickname such as Grey Steel
3. Like a simple form of worship
4. Wear plain clothes
5. Be very serious

Royalists:

1. Support the Stuart Kings
2. Think the King should have total power
3. Like lots of ceremony in church
4. Wear swashbuckling clothes
5. Love having parties

John Knox was a famous preacher. He was also **rather dour**. He visited Castle Campbell in 1556 and gave an outdoor sermon.

And another thing: stop watching plays, singing, and having a good time

Did you know?
Castle Campbell is also home to many bats who roost at the top of the tower.

DR MACBANE'S REMEDIES

Hi. I'm Dr MacBane. How are you feeling? Not good? Then let me make you better

Try some of my special cures

To stop a wound bleeding
Smear it with hog's dung.

A bad headache
Place 10 leeches upon your forehead. Let them suck your blood until you feel better.

Bad cough
Take 2 or 3 snails, ½ cup of barley and 4 cups of water. Boil them all up and strain. Take 2 spoonfuls of liquid to stop coughing.

Jaundice
Swallow 9 lice every morning.

Inflamed eyelid
Try rubbing your eyelid with the tail of a black cat.

To relieve fever
Mix ox dung with half a scruple of masterwort. Boil in a pan of water. Strain the liquid and drink.

Scrofula
Get a member of the Stuart royal family to touch you.

To stop a nose bleed
Tie a frog around your neck.

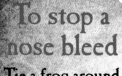

These are all real remedies from the past!

Did you know?
Some children got scrofula from cows' milk, in the days when cows were often diseased. It affected the children's throats and lungs. Many parents gave their children small ale (very weak beer) to drink instead

USEFUL POTIONS YOU CAN MAKE AT HOME

Here's some old remedies for you to try

To clean your teeth
Rub your teeth with fresh strawberries

For a relaxing bath:

Heat 2 jugfuls of water.
Add the leaves of lemon balm, borage and sage, and some rose petals.
Strain the liquid and pour into a warm bath.

To cure a cold

Ingredients
Spoonful of honey
Juice of ½ lemon
Pinch of thyme
½ cup of hot water

Mix. Cool. Drink.

To soothe a headache

Dab a little rosewater on your forehead. Lie in a dark room for half an hour.

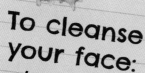

To cleanse your face:

Ingredients
Cup of creamy milk
Fine oatmeal
Chopped mixed herbs

Mix together and smooth onto face.
Leave for 15 minutes.

A hair rinse (to make it shine):

ingredients
FOR FAIR HAIR: CAMOMILE FLOWERS
FOR DARK HAIR: LAVENDER FLOWERS
FOR LIGHT BROWN HAIR:
MARJORAM LEAVES
FOR RED HAIR: SAGE LEAVES

SCONE PALACE 1651

SCONE IS NOW A STATELY HOME BUT IT WAS ONCE THE PLACE OF CORONATIONS. IN 1651, CHARLES STUART WAS CROWNED KING CHARLES II AT SCONE.

Charles had been in exile since his father (Charles I) had been beheaded in London. Oliver Cromwell now ruled England but, in Scotland, the Covenanters held sway. The Covenanter, Archibald Campbell, invited Charles to Scotland. Archibald was a very powerful man and Charles didn't trust him!

WHY I DON'T TRUST ARCHIBALD, BY CHARLES STUART:

1. IT WAS HIS MEN WHO HANDED MY DAD TO THE ENGLISH (AND THEY CHOPPED OFF HIS HEAD).
2. HE DOESN'T LIKE ME HAVING A GOOD TIME.
3 HE TUTS A LOT (WHICH IS VERY ANNOYING).
4. WHO'S TO SAY HE WON'T CHOP OFF MY HEAD?
STILL I WOULD LIKE TO BE KING....

MINISTER, ROBERT DOUGLAS

ARCHIBALD CAMPBELL, 1ST MARQUESS OF ARGYLL

Are we going to be nice to him?

LAST MONARCH TO BE CROWNED AT SCONE

I hope this is a good idea

And, um another thing...

The sermon lasted a very long time!

What happened next?

Oliver Cromwell invaded Scotland. Charles fought back and led his Scottish regiments into England but was defeated in a big battle at Worcester. Charles hid in a famous oak tree before fleeing back to Europe.

Archibald Campbell then became pals with Cromwell. But, in 1660, Charles returned and was crowned king of both Scotland and England. The next year, Archibald was beheaded for treason.

Back in 1306, Robert the Bruce had a quick coronation at Scone shortly after murdering his rival. There was no time to get the royal crown so he used a golden circlet instead. His sister Isabel crowned him.

She was a very useful sister. Bet you wish you had a sister like that.

Lots of Scottish kings were crowned on this stone.

It came to Scone from Dalriada in 843

Edward I stole it in 1296

Charles II used it in 1660 – in Westminster Abbey!

Moot Hill

Moot Hill at Scone is also called Boot Hill. It's said that, once upon a time, the nobles had to swear their loyalty before the king while standing on their own land. Since the king couldn't travel to all their homes, they stored a bit of earth in their boots and brought it along to Scone. Then they poured the earth before their king and stood on it! Eventually, these offerings created a small hill.

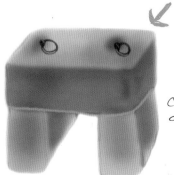

Did you know?

The famous Coronation Stone of Scone is now in Edinburgh Castle

DUNNOTTAR CASTLE 1651-60

DUNNOTTAR CASTLE STANDS ON CLIFFS HIGH ABOVE THE SEA. IT WAS ONCE A PLACE WHERE PRINCES COULD STAY. CHARLES STUART LODGED THERE BEFORE BEING CROWNED KING CHARLES II, AT SCONE.

FOR THE CORONATION, THE **CROWN JEWELS** WERE BROUGHT FROM EDINBURGH. BUT THEN OLIVER CROMWELL INVADED SCOTLAND AND **TOOK CONTROL OF THE CAPITAL CITY...**

The Crown Jewels

Cromwell wanted to get rid of all kings and rule the whole of Britain. But he needed money to fund his republic. Once in Edinburgh, he looked for the Scottish crown jewels (the 'Honours of Scotland'). He'd already broken up the English crown jewels and sold the precious stones. Now he wanted the Scottish ones.

But the Scottish jewels had been taken to Dunnottar Castle. Cromwell ordered his troops to Dunnottar where they besieged the castle for eight months. Cannons were finally brought in to bombard the walls, and the troops broke through to the castle rooms. At once, they demanded the crown jewels. But they had disappeared!

Squawk!

plop

Ye wee besom!

Tum-te -tum...

MRS GRAINGER (WIFE OF THE MINISTER AT KINEFF)

D'ye think we'll ever get into that castle?

Did you know?

The castle was once held by Edaurd I of England but, in 1296, William Wallace won it back. The next year, he beat Edward's army at the Battle of Stirling Bridge

Where were they?

It's said that the local minister's wife lowered the crown jewels in a creel to her maid, who was waiting on the shore. She then hid the King's private papers **under her skirt** and slipped past Cromwell's soldiers.

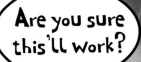

Are you sure this'll work?

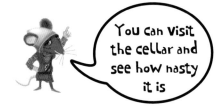

Och, you'll be fine. Pretend you're collecting seaweed

What happened next?

The jewels were **hidden** beneath the floor of Kineff Kirk, until King Charles returned to Britain in 1660.

The Killing Time

When King Charles II ruled Scotland and England (after 1660), he was **very mean** to the Covenanters. The period was called the Killing Time. In 1685, 167 men and women were imprisoned in the cellar at Dunnottar because they didn't support the king. Some died. Some agreed to support him, after all. The rest were sent to the West Indian plantations as **slaves**.

You can visit the cellar and see how nasty it is

URQUHART CASTLE 1692

URQUHART CASTLE IS THE VERY BEST PLACE TO SPOT NESSIE!

PEOPLE HAVE LIVED ON THE SITE FOR MANY HUNDREDS OF YEARS, INCLUDING (PROBABLY) THE CELTS AND (DEFINITELY) THE PICTS. D'YOU RECKON ANY OF THEM SAW NESSIE?

In its heyday, the castle was one of the largest in Scotland with a huge gatehouse, a keep and a citadel. Its history was a bit like lots of Scottish castles:

1. Built and **attacked**, extended and **attacked**, strengthened and **attacked**.
2. Held by the English during the Wars of Independence, but Robert the Bruce got it back again.
3. Set upon by various Scottish clans who didn't like whoever was living there at the time.
4. The Covenanters turned up in 1644.
5. Cromwell's men arrived a few years later BUT ignored the castle and instead of attacking it, they built a new fort at each end of the loch.

A small garrison lived at the castle but by 1692, it was in poor repair. The soldiers were told to leave. Before going they blew up the castle so no one else could us it!

50

Much of the castle is in ruins... Have you ever wondered happened to all those stones?

BLAIR CASTLE 1746

BLAIR LOOKS LIKE A **FAIRYTALE CASTLE**. IT HAS A RICH HISTORY. IT WAS HERE THAT THE LAST CASTLE SIEGE IN BRITAIN TOOK PLACE!

Away with you

SIR ANDREW AGNEW (SUPPORTER OF THE DUKE)

In 1745, Bonnie Prince Charlie (BPC) landed in Scotland. He was there to lead the Jacobite Rebellion. King George II was on the throne – but BPC thought his father, James Francis Stuart, should be there instead.

The Jacobite Rebellion split families apart. At Blair Castle, the clan chief (2nd Duke of Atholl) supported King George. But most of the clan preferred BPC, including the chief's brother (Lord George Murray).

In 1746, when Government soldiers were staying at Blair Castle, Lord George appeared with a troop of Jacobites. He demanded that the soldiers surrendered with all their supplies. When they refused, his men lay siege to the castle.

I demand you surrender!

LORD GEORGE →

Ah'm thinking this isnae working

What happened next?

The Jacobites left to join BPC and fight at the **Battle of Culloden.**
They were defeated and many of the men died. Lord George and BPC escaped to France. The garrison of men at Blair also fought at Culloden, on the side of King George II. They won the battle.

How to be an Ideal Jacobite in 1746:

1. Support Bonnie Prince Charlie and his dad, James Francis Stuart
2. Hate King George II and the Government army
3. Be a Highlander
4. Be Catholic
5. Wear a kilt, and look sort of wild and romantic

BPC had some Lowland, English and Protestant supporters, too though!

Happy Days

Mary Queen of Scots stayed at Blair in 1564. A special hunt was arranged for her, and over **300 deer and 5 wolves were killed.**

Queen Victoria stayed for three weeks in 1844. She had such a good time that she later **bought Balmoral Castle -** so she could keep returning to Scotland.

WHO WERE THE JACOBITES?

KING JAMES VII (AND II OF ENGLAND) WASN'T VERY POPULAR SO WHEN HE HAD A SON, INSTEAD OF REJOICING, EVERYONE GOT CROSS. THIS WAS BECAUSE THEY DIDN'T WANT HIS SON TO BECOME THE NEXT KING. FEELING THAT NO ONE LIKED HIM, JAMES FLED TO FRANCE.

His daughter Mary ruled Britain instead, along with her husband (and cousin) William.

But not everyone was pleased about this either. A whole bunch of people thought James' son should be King. James' son became known as the Old Pretender. He was also called James. His supporters were called Jacobites. They kept having Uprisings.

Many Scottish clansmen gathered to fight for BPC (though some clans supported the British Government army instead). BPC did very well at first and invaded England but, when he got to Derby, he decided there weren't enough soldiers to attack London.

BPC gained less support in England than he'd expected (though the Manchester regiment fought for him). The promised French army did not arrive, either. In the end, his troops marched back to Scotland. In April 1746, the Jacobite army was destroyed at the Battle of Culloden.

In 1745, the Old Pretender's son came to Scotland to fight for his father's right to rule Britain. He was the Young Pretender – also known as Bonnie Prince Charlie (BPC).

By the time BPC arrived, there had been three more rulers on the British throne. The latest one was King George II, from Hanover. (He was the great-great-great-great-grandson of Mary Queen of Scots.) But the supporters of BPC liked him even less than William and Mary.

What happened next?

BPC escaped (disguised as a lady's maid) to Skye and then to France.

Many of his supporters were killed. Some were sent to galley ships or to slave plantations. Others escaped but had to live in exile.

The wearing of tartan was banned for 36 years.

Did you know?
Jacobite comes from Latin for James (Jacobus)

SECRET SIGNS AND CODES

BOTH THE JACOBITE AND BRITISH GOVERNMENT ARMIES HAD SPIES. THE JACOBITES ALSO HAD LOTS OF SECRET SIGNS, SUCH AS THE WHITE COCKADE AND THE OAK LEAF. THEY CAN BE VERY USEFUL. WHY NOT CHOOSE YOUR OWN SECRET SIGN?

Codes are very useful too.
Here are 3 different codes that you can try:

Code 1:

Use the grid to work out each letter in the message.

	1	2	3	4	5
1	A	B	C	D	E
2	F	G	H	I	J
3	K	L	M	N	O
4	P	Q	R	S	T
5	U	V	W	X	Y/Z

The message:
33 15 15 45
11 45
45 23 15
23 11 43 12 35 51 43

Can you work out these messages?

Code 2: YPSYM ENEDE RUTPA CEVAH

Code 3: RDMC LNQD SQNNOR

Invisible Ink:

You can write your messages in invisible ink. Try using vinegar. You'll need an old-fashioned dip pen – or a small stick (such as a used matchstick) – for writing. Write your message and leave it to dry. To see the words, gently heat the paper.

Code 3 (Write down the alphabet. Then shift each letter in the message once to the left): Send more troops

Answers: Code 1: Meet me at the harbour. Code 2 (Message written backwards, with the letters in sets of 5): Have captured enemy spy.

55

INVERARAY CASTLE 1776

CLAN CAMPBELL WAS A POWERFUL CLAN. THE CAMPBELLS WERE BOTH FEARED AND ADMIRED, DEPENDING ON WHICH SIDE YOU WERE ON.

For hundreds of years, clans feuded against each other but, in the later 1700s, things became more peaceful. In 1746, the Campbell chief, the Duke of Argyll, decided to build a new home. He was fed up with his old fortified castle in the middle of a loch. So he looked around the area and found a perfect site for a new castle, right next to the sea. In those days, people travelled a lot by sea - so being near it was a good idea.

Since he was getting a posh new house, the Duke thought he'd give his tenants nice new homes too. Or, to put it another way: stinky old Inveraray village was ruining his view - so he decided to move the village. Starting in 1746, the castle took 43 years to finish! The town took quite a while, too. Most of the villagers had time to get used to the idea — but maybe not all of them.

TENEMENTS WERE BUILT FOR THE POORER PEOPLE IN 1776.

His Lordship's given you a brand new home. What's not to like?

Och, they're very nice

Aye, they look fine to me

Ah preferr'd ma auld hovel where ah was born

Elephant Polo

The Duke of Argyll has represented Scotland in elephant polo matches. (The game began in Nepal in 1982.) This is how it's played:

There are two people on each elephant (one playing and one trying to control the elephant). There are four elephants on each team. Each player tries to hit a ball into the goal, using a very long stick.

Sometimes the elephants cheat. There are penalties for lying in front of the goal or leaving the pitch to eat bamboo. Cheating is better than getting cross though. One elephant in Sri Lanka threw its riders before trashing a parked minibus. He was banned from the game.

Do you think this sport should be in the Olympics?

INVERARAY CASTLE TODAY

I wish I was at home

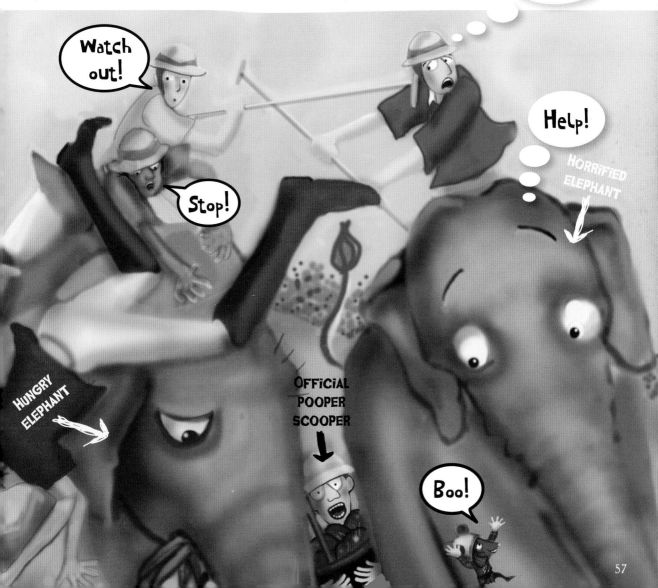

57

CULZEAN CASTLE WAS BUILT IN THE LATE 1700s THE 10TH EARL OF CASSILLIS (BUT THERE'S A MUCH OLDER TOWER HOUSE WITHIN IT). THE NEW GEORGIAN MANSION WAS THE VERY LATEST THING, DESIGNED BY TOP ARCHITECT ROBERT ADAM. IT HAD LOVELY ROOMS, PAINTED CEILINGS, AN AMAZING STAIRCASE AND ALL MOD CONS — WITH RUNNING WATER (TAPS) AND WATER CLOSETS (TOILETS) ON EVERY FLOOR.

IT TOOK 15 YEARS TO BUILD, AND WAS ALL FOR ONE MAN SO HE COULD SHOW OFF TO HIS FRIENDS AND HAVE GREAT PARTIES. SADLY, THE EARL DIED BEFORE IT WAS QUITE FINISHED. HE PROBABLY HAD SOME GOOD TIMES, THOUGH.

How about this wig?

DAVID KENNEDY, 10TH EARL OF CASSILLIS, GETTING READY FOR A PARTY.

The Earl was very friendly, but some of his ancestors were not so nice. For instance, one of them roasted an abbot.

The Roasting of the Abbot

In 1560, it became **illegal to be a Catholic.** Over the next ten years, the Reformers (or Protestants) sacked a lot of Catholic abbeys, taking all their gold and other nice things. But, instead of sacking Crossraguel Abbey, near Culzean, they put in their own 'abbot'. The abbot managed the rich abbey farms and sent all the profits to his masters.

ONE OF EARL'S HENCHMEN.

No!

ABBOT

The 4th Earl of Cassillis was furious. He hated the Reformers, and wanted the abbey lands and wealth for himself. So he tried to **bribe** the abbot. He offered him money if he'd give him the lands. When the abbot refused, the Earl threatened him. But this didn't work either. So then the Earl took the abbot to one of his dungeons and roasted him over a fire. His younger brother, Sir Thomas of Culzean, helped him.

What happened next?

After being **roasted twice**, the abbot signed a document saying the Earl could have all the lands. But once he was free, he told everyone what had happened and they all thought the Earl was **really mean**. So the Earl had to give the lands back again. Later, though, he bought them legally (who would dare touch them?). They're still part of the Kennedy estate.

Culzean is pronounced Kull-ane. And Cassillis sounds like Kassels!

Just say you'll give us the abbey lands

THOMAS ↗

EARL ↗

Oh, for goodness sake...

CRATHES CASTLE c.1845

CRATHES WAS OWNED BY THE BURNETT FAMILY FOR MANY YEARS. THEY HAD FOUGHT VERY HARD FOR ROBERT THE BRUCE AND SO HE GAVE THEM SOME LAND. IN 1553, THE BURNETTS BUILT A LOVELY NEW STONE CASTLE. THE CASTLE WAS A FAMILY HOME WITH COMFORTABLE ROOMS AND NICE PAINTED CEILINGS. BUT, AT SOME POINT IN ITS HISTORY, SOMETHING VERY SAD HAPPENED.

The Lady and the Skeleton

Within the castle is the Green Lady's Room. It's called that because, sometimes, a lady dressed in green can be seen walking across the room with a baby in her arms. Then she disappears.

In Victorian times, some workmen found a skeleton beneath the hearth stone, in that same room. The skeleton was of an infant child. Why was it buried there? No one knows. But, perhaps the Green Lady keeps returning to Crathes to find her baby.

What do you think?

Och, how sad

The poor wee thing

Here's your chance to add your thoughts:

It's good to have friends in high places

Most castles got attacked - but the Burnetts did things differently. During the Wars of Religion, in 1644, the Marquess of Montrose turned up at Crathes with a troop of men and demanded to take the castle. Sir Thomas Burnett agreed!

He then invited Montrose to dinner. They got on very well. After their meal, they relaxed and chatted over a few drinks. So relaxed was Montrose that, the next day, he rode away leaving the castle in the care of Sir Thomas.

I think the Green Lady..... is sad

If you like Green Ladies, there's one at Fyvie too!

FYVIE CASTLE MODERN DAY

Since around 1390, five different families have owned Fyvie. Each family has added a tower to the castle!

In 1885, Alexander Forbes-Leith bought the castle for £175,000 (and added the final tower).

The castle is beautiful. But **watch out** for the **Green Lady**.

Can you work out the names of the other families who owned Fyvie?

PR- preston

1. Notserp
2. Murdlem *meldrum*
3. Notes *seton*
4. Nodrog *gordon*

Think backwards

The Green Lady of Fyvie

For many years, Lilias Drummond was the wife of Alexander Seton. She bore him **five daughters** but **no sons.** Each time a baby daughter arrived, her husband became angry. Alexander wanted a son who could inherit Fyvie and carry on his family name.

Lilias became very sad and hid herself away. She grew thin and wan. Then one day, she died. No one was sure what had happened. Some thought that her husband had grown tired of her and she'd died of a **broken** heart. But others whispered that poor Lilias had been locked into a room and **starved** to death! Whatever the truth, Alexander soon took a second wife.

One night, when the newly married couple retired to bed, they heard a strange **SCRATCHING SOUND** outside their window. In the morning, the words 'D. LILIAS DRUMMOND' were found carved into the window sill.

Lilias still appears at Fyvie now and again. She wanders down the staircase and through the hall, still the mistress of the house. Sometimes, before she appears, there is beautiful **smell** of roses.

Do you want a banana?